HEADMISTRESS PRESS BOOKS

Fireworks in the Graveyard - Joy Ladin
Social Dance - Carolyn Boll
The Force of Gratitude - Janice Gould
Spine - Sarah Caulfield
Diatribe from the Library - Farrell Greenwald Brenner
Blind Girl Grunt - Constance Merritt
Acid and Tender - Jen Rouse
Beautiful Machinery - Wendy DeGroat
Odd Mercy - Gail Thomas
The Great Scissor Hunt - Jessica K. Hylton
A Bracelet of Honeybees - Lynn Strongin
Whirlwind @ Lesbos - Risa Denenberg
The Body's Alphabet - Ann Tweedy
First name Barbie last name Doll - Maureen Bocka
Heaven to Me - Abe Louise Young
Sticky - Carter Steinmann
Tiger Laughs When You Push - Ruth Lehrer
Night Ringing - Laura Foley
Paper Cranes - Dinah Dietrich
A Crown of Violets - Renée Vivien tr. Samantha Pious
On Loving a Saudi Girl - Carina Yun
The Burn Poems - Lynn Strongin
I Carry My Mother - Lesléa Newman
Distant Music - Joan Annsfire
The Awful Suicidal Swans - Flower Conroy
Joy Street - Laura Foley
Chiaroscuro Kisses - G.L. Morrison
The Lillian Trilogy - Mary Meriam
Lady of the Moon - Amy Lowell, Lillian Faderman, Mary Meriam
Irresistible Sonnets - ed. Mary Meriam

LAVENDER REVIEW

LAVENDER REVIEW

Poems from the First Five Years

Edited by

MARY MERIAM

Headmistress Press

Copyright © 2015 Lavender Review and Mary Meriam.
All rights reserved. This book may not be reproduced, in whole or in part, including illustrations, in any form (beyond that permitted by Sections 107 and 108 of the U.S. Copyright Law and except by reviewers for the public press), without written permission from the publishers.

ISBN-13: 978-0692356210
ISBN-10: 0692356215
ISSN: 2168-537 (online)

Cover Art © 2008 Leslie Satterfield, *I thought she was mine (2)*. "89" © 2008 Suzanne Gardinier, *Today: 101 Ghazals* (Sheep Meadow Press).
"for tender stalkes (12)" © 2015 Roger Mitchell for the estate of Catherine Breese Davis.
"Granting Passage" © 2014 Flower Conroy, *The Awful Suicidal Swans* (Headmistress Press).
"Recital" © 2013 Rick Mullin, *Coelancanth* (Dos Madres Press).
"Some Sleep Deeper" © 1992 Suzanne J. Doyle, *Dangerous Beauties* (Margery Cantor Press).
"The Oasis" © 2012 Naomi Replansky, *Collected Poems* (Black Sparrow Press).

Cover & book design by Mary Meriam.

PUBLISHER
Headmistress Press
60 Shipview Lane
Sequim, WA 98382
Telephone: 917-428-8312
Email: headmistresspress@gmail.com
Website: headmistresspress.blogspot.com

For Lesbian Poets,
Past, Present, and Future

CONTENTS

Preface

ALIX GREENWOOD
Night   1

ALYSE KNORR
Stellar Era Ends   2
May Support Life   3

AMY LEVY
A Wall Flower   4

AMY LOWELL
The Letter   5
The Weather-Cock Points South   6

ANDREA DULANTO
Dear Virginia   7

ANN TWEEDY
swimming through history   9

CATHERINE BREESE DAVIS
for tender stalkes (12)   12

CHARLOTTE MEW
There shall be no night there In the Fields   13
Absence   14

CHRISTINA ROSSETTI
A Bird Song   15
from *Sing-Song, A Nursery Rhyme Book*   16

COLLEEN McKEE
In the Glossy Green Heart of the Neighborhood   17

E.F. SCHRAEDER
Government Cheese   18

Eleanor Lerman
Beloved   19
For the Stay-At-Home Wife   20

Flower Conroy
Granting Passage   21

Hannah Baker-Siroty
That One Dream—the Quick of Me.   23
Up Here Where the Heat Rises   24

Holly Mitchell
We Need the Boat of Love, Not the Boat of Tolerance 25

J.K. Daniels
Genealogy   26

Janice Gould
Waking in the Dark   27
Gacela of Bamboo and Plum Blossoms   28

Joy Ladin
Balance   30
How Much   31

Judy Grahn
Magda: 32

Lady Mary Wortley Montagu
Farewell to Bath   34

Laura Foley
I Go Down to the River   36

Lesléa Newman
I Want to Stay Up Talking But   37
Paradise Found   38

Marina Tsvetaeva
from Podruga (Friend)   39

Marty McConnell
Object 41

Marva Zohar
Our Winter 43

Mary Elizabeth Coleridge
The Witch 46

Mary Kathryn Arnold
Christine 47

Mia
The Dog Lover 48

Minnie Bruce Pratt
The Moon, Reading 50
The Wood Thrush Sings 51

Naomi Replansky
The Oasis 52

Nicole Brossard
[brushing the song in you] 53

O. Ayes
called rush 54

R. Nemo Hill
The Girls Are In The Trees 55
From A Man To The Youth He Loves 56

Rachel Rose
A Wedding Ghazal 57

Renée Vivien
Sappho's Disdain 58

Rick Mullin
Recital 59

RISA DENENBERG
Yellow Star   60
Before World   61

RITA MAE REESE
At 36, Hulga Speaks of Love   62

ROBIN BECKER
The Black Bear Inside Me   64

ROSE KELLEHER
Compensation   66

SARA TEASDALE
Since There Is No Escape   67
September Midnight   68

SARAH SARAI
Longing for a Blue Sky   69
This Way and That   70

SHAWNDRA MILLER
Freeze Warning, April 10   72
Blackbird   74

SOPHIE JEWETT
Defeated   75

SUZANNE J. DOYLE
Some Sleep Deeper   76

SUZANNE GARDINIER
89   77

TIMOTHY MURPHY
An Old Man Speaks   79

About the Poets   81

ABOUT THE EDITOR

Poet Mary Meriam is the founder of *Lavender Review,* co-founder of Headmistress Press, editor of *Irresistible Sonnets,* and author of *The Countess of Flatbroke, The Poet's Zodiac,* and *The Lillian Trilogy (Word Hot, Conjuring My Leafy Muse,* and *Girlie Calendar).* She contributes essays, reviews, and interviews to *Ms.* Magazine Blog and *The Gay & Lesbian Review.*

ABOUT THE PUBLISHER

Headmistress Press is an independent publisher of books of poetry by lesbians. As a small press, Headmistress is dedicated to honoring lesbian existence, discovering a range of lesbian voices, and promoting lesbian representation in the arts.

PREFACE

So now you hold in your hot hands poems from the first five years (ten issues) of my solo-run e-zine, *Lavender Review*. Born on Gay Pride Day, 2010, *Lavender Review* is an international, biannual e-zine dedicated to poetry and art by, about, and for lesbians, including whatever might appeal to a lesbian readership. This is *Lavender Review's* first foray into print. True, you can read all the poems online for free at **lavrev.net** but some of us love to hold a book in our hands.

The 48 contributors to this anthology include renowned and new lesbian poets; translations of Marina Tsvetaeva, Renée Vivien, and Sappho; some poems from the past by Amy Lowell, Charlotte Mew, Sara Teasdale, and others; and a few lesbian-friendly poems by straight and gay poets.

Many thanks to the poets and artists who have contributed their dazzling poems and artwork to my e-zine these past five years. I love all of you and your work, and of course, none of this could have happened without you. Many thanks also to my backers over the years, whose generosity helps keep *Lavender Review* alive.

Mary Meriam
January, 2015

Any art from a marginalized group is first dismissed as necessarily trivial or lesser because it doesn't value the same ideals as the mainstream. It is only through iteration and resilience that the markers used to keep us out become the elements for which we are prized. That's why a journal devoted to lesbian poetry and art is vital: it rejects tokenism; it makes visible the common themes between otherwise dissimilar writers and artists; and, most importantly, it shows the range and prowess of those who would otherwise be limited to one feature of their work.

—Eloise Stonborough

ALIX GREENWOOD

Night

Silence known by the light tap
Of rain, of after-rain
Shedding from leaves.
Night known by the star outside,
And dark clouds rimmed
By the less-dark sky.
The day known
By its uncoiling down through cells,
Slowly, into silence and night.
Body known by the press of cover
On limb, of limb on sheet,
On bed, on soil and rock and Earth.
None of it to last, not silence
Or night, or cloud or star,
Or day or body or planet;
Silence a ring I have made
Against cars and planes;
Night a contrivance
Against surrounding light.

ALYSE KNORR

Stellar Era Ends

Our hands find each other even now, in this growing dark.
Somehow, your light reaches me and spreads its
Opal brilliance into my bones, into my
Open mouth. To say that we have lived to see this—but there will be
No one to tell. Of mornings in the garden, kissing your
Neck and smelling basil and earth and sweat.
Only now can we rejoice in this great
Wholeness, this great death.
My life has consisted of a handful of pulsings, of
Years waiting for this time—the time of
Losing all light, losing
Ourselves, and the
Very memory of
Everything else.

May Support Life

Double the size of the Earth, 600 light years away,
Kepler 22-b has the climate of a balmy Key West day.
Fleck on a telescope, wobbled light in a star's pinprick,
caught like a small bee in the snare of a child's net.
In the artist's depiction, Kepler 22-b looks modest,
embarrassed, even—cloud-swirled sky bowing down
at a tilt in the painted nebula. NASA named it after
the telescope that found it.
                              If I had a planet, I would
resist the urge to name it at all. My planet would drag
moons to it like great weights at the ends of large coiling
chains. Its years would last days and its days, years.
The oceans of my planet—there would be only oceans,
no land—would slither with possibility and pull back
and forth with the tides of many, many moons. And with
each grand, sweeping arc around its sun—which would
also, of course, remain nameless—my planet would pick up
speed—enough to hurl itself out of the solar system
and toward a planet blinking in the distance behind a lens
the size of a skyscraper—a planet staring up, taking notes,
looking for a new habitable zone as the end hurtles dead ahead.

AMY LEVY

A Wall Flower

*I lounge in the doorway and languish in vain
While Tom, Dick and Harry are dancing with Jane*

My spirit rises to the music's beat;
There is a leaden fiend lurks in my feet!
To move unto your motion, Love, were sweet.

Somewhere, I think, some other where, not here,
In other ages, on another sphere,
I danced with you, and you with me, my dear.

In perfect motion did our bodies sway,
To perfect music that was heard alway;
Woe's me, that am so dull of foot to-day!

To move unto your motion, Love, were sweet;
My spirit rises to the music's beat—
But, ah, the leaden demon in my feet!

AMY LOWELL

The Letter

Little cramped words scrawling all over the paper
Like draggled fly's legs,
What can you tell of the flaring moon
Through the oak leaves?
Or of my curtained window and the bare floor
Spattered with moonlight?
Your silly quirks and twists have nothing in them
Of blossoming hawthorns,
And this paper is dull, crisp, smooth, virgin of loveliness
Beneath my hand.

I am tired, Beloved, of chafing my heart against
The want of you;
Of squeezing it into little inkdrops,
And posting it.
And I scald alone, here, under the fire
Of the great moon.

The Weather-Cock Points South

I put your leaves aside,
One by one:
The stiff, broad outer leaves;
The smaller ones,
Pleasant to touch, veined with purple;
The glazed inner leaves.
One by one
I parted you from your leaves,
Until you stood up like a white flower
Swaying slightly in the evening wind.

White flower,
Flower of wax, of jade, of unstreaked agate;
Flower with surfaces of ice,
With shadows faintly crimson.
Where in all the garden is there such a flower?
The stars crowd through like lilac leaves
To look at you.
The low moon brightens you with silver.

The bud is more than the calyx.
There is nothing to equal a white bud,
Of no colour, and of all,
Burnished by moonlight,
Thrust upon by a softly-swinging wind.

ANDREA DULANTO

Dear Virginia

when you wrote about prunes and custard
and said we should strive for the highest art
without giving into
the sour pudding
of our lives,
did you really think that was possible?

Because you did gather stones into your pockets
and kneel down to madness
between breakfast and tea
with your chatter of voices:

> *Not good enough,*
> *Virginia!*

> *You were lucky this time,*
> *Virginia!*

> *No more words left,*
> *Virginia!*

Pale in your nightgown
but you knew your own worth—
you knew
when you were writing your books—
no child can compare to this.

Yes,
incandescence

Yes,
death to the sitting-room
where Jane Austen hides her manuscripts
whenever she hears someone walking down the hall

No more crippled works,
nothing that spews—
    women, hold your venom—(not likely)
the obsession with a work
    expressed completely—(written between breakfast and
        tea and madness)

voices-in-your-head
    be damned—
we are crippled, Virginia,

we are crippled
and we walk on water.

ANN TWEEDY

swimming through history

i. the truckee and the skagit

ankle-deep in summertime, the truckee
lets you climb down and taste it,
but the wide, deep skagit
demands a firmer commitment.

ii. learning the skagit

at home, when i'm getting more
than a glimpse through a car window,
i'm walking the dike
above the skagit, kingly or queenly,
the way dutch farmers devised it.
glancing, these downstream waters
look still as a painting, linger in one spot,
yet the whole mass rushes.

but once, upstream in early
december, i watched the last chum
undulate in slow motion, their bodies
ripped by so many rocks
in their against-current trek
that blood streaked them. only
a few swam; the rest floated. the sight
made the toil of sisyphus

look easy. another time, i saw the tiny
nearly finless body of a juvenile
barely larger than a tadpole, stranded
on the beach at deception pass.
the silver body throbbed at the gill
while the oversized eye stared upward.
when i cupped the fingerling in my hands
to throw it back to sea, it flopped
down to escape me.

still, all my looking makes
just a drop next to the hours
i sit and write brief after brief
to keep more water in the banks
during the months when the skagit
is lowest or negotiate day in,
day out for salmon to have more water
to spawn and rear in, only to find myself
lost and cut off. i long to squish
my fingers and toes in mud or throw
my body headlong into current.
what wisdoms and strengths would the river
feed me if i could let myself go?
but how to face the great surge of life,
bearing effort that may come to nothing?

iii. visiting the truckee

yesterday, remembering all this, i climbed
down to the truckee. here and there, logs made
crevices where adult fish could build redds.
i lay on a rock and let the river tug my feet
feeling how easily it could crush my unnimble
body on the rocks. i peered at the little pools

along the sides of the banks, and saw how the sun
shining through slower ripples
made a pulsing snakeskin pattern. i thought of the newly
hatched fry who might shelter there

except that—thanks to the dam and other
interference—the lahontan cutthroat
who ruled these reaches were killed off
more than sixty years ago.
now, stocked trout and ghosts swim here.

CATHERINE BREESE DAVIS

for tender stalkes

12.

Sleepless, I think: how I should sleep
Cradled, as once, all night and eased
Of all the anguish that I keep
Pent up, alone, awake, diseased.

But then I think how restless I
Have been with love, how I would toss
And turn, would, though with love, still lie
Alone, possessed by an unknown loss.

It is not lack of love that left us
Sad as Simonides, whose sadness
Never embraced this unloved madness
That let the thought of such loss war
With having, which grief has bereft us
Of peace. But that is where we are.

CHARLOTTE MEW

There shall be no night there
In the Fields

Across these wind-blown meadows I can see
    The far off glimmer of the little town,
    And feel the darkness slowly shutting down
To lock from day's long glare my soul and me.
    Then through my blood the coming mystery
Of night steals to my heart and turns my feet
Toward that chamber in the lamp-lit street,
    Where waits the pillow of thy breast and thee.

'There shall be no night there' —no curtained pane
    To shroud love's speechlessness and loose thy hair
For kisses swift and sweet as falling rain.
    No soft release of life—no evening prayer.
    Nor shall we waking greet the dawn, aware
That with the darkness we may sleep again.

Absence

Sometimes I know the way
    You walk, up over the bay;
It is a wind from the far sea
That blows the fragrance of your hair to me.

Or in this garden when the breeze
    Touches my trees
To stir their dreaming shadows on the grass
    I see you pass.

In sheltered beds, the heart of every rose
    Serenely sleeps tonight. As shut as those
Your guarded heart; as safe as they from the beat, beat
Of hooves that tread dropped roses in the street.

    Turn never again
    On these eyes blind with a wild rain
Your eyes; they were stars to me.—
There are things stars may not see.

But call, call, and though Christ stands
    Still with scarred hands
Over my mouth, I must answer. So
I will come—He shall let me go!

CHRISTINA ROSSETTI

A Bird Song

It's a year almost that I have not seen her:
Oh, last summer green things were greener,
Brambles fewer, the blue sky bluer.

It's surely summer, for there's a swallow:
Come one swallow, his mate will follow,
The bird race quicken and wheel and thicken.

Oh happy swallow whose mate will follow
O'er height, o'er hollow! I'd be a swallow,
To build this weather one nest together.

from *Sing-Song, A Nursery Rhyme Book*

A rose has thorns as well as honey,
I'll not have her for love or money;
An iris grows so straight and fine,
That she shall be no friend of mine;
Snowdrops like the snow would chill me;
Nightshade would caress and kill me;
Crocus like a spear would fright me;
Dragon's-mouth might bark or bite me;
Convolvulus but blooms to die;
A wind-flower suggests a sigh;
Love-lies-bleeding makes me sad;
And poppy-juice would drive me mad:—
But give me holly, bold and jolly,
Honest, prickly, shining holly;
Pluck me holly leaf and berry
For the day when I make merry.

COLLEEN MCKEE

In the Glossy Green Heart of the Neighborhood

We quarreled up Washington, Waterman, Ames,
through the elegant gated boulevards,
"communities" where we did not belong.

From behind trimmed hedges, good homeowners
glowered at us, two plump girls
in shabby skirts cooing, sniffing,
humidly clutching, then releasing
each others' hands, blowing our noses
on crumpled Kleenex, declaring our love and dismay
loudly enough for the neighbors to hear,
and you know, it's one thing…but as long
as you keep it behind closed doors…

But our salaries did not permit privacy,
only roommates who multiplied like mice,
so in the glossy green heart of the neighborhood
I pilfered a zinnia the color of brick
worrying, bending the fibrous stalk,
felt a sting as my fingers slid down the stem
from the slender short hairs that looked soft as yours.

The leaves stiff as paper said, promise,
I promise. It did not want to give,
but I gave it to you.

E.F. SCHRAEDER

Government Cheese

I come from a long line of loud dressers, masters of
second-hand cool reinvention in paisley shirts,
checked sweaters, and striped pants.

So if it's true that we, my family and I, weren't poor
it's in the same way that later I wasn't homeless.
It's a matter of surface attention, directed awareness.

I slipped between friendly couches, a queer kid
without a home. I learned denial like that
from Mom. She emptied illusions in her free time:

poured samples into larger shampoo bottles, softened
soap shavings with water into batches of liquid
cleanser to rinse away our hidden poverty.

I knew who I was, backpack slung over one arm
clomping out of the house. We are two versions of a story
that end the same. Even alienated, I am half of her.

I learned to need less, become my own brand.
Half of what we are is accident, luck. The other, creativity.
To have enough of everything, we practiced frugality:

laughed at the gooey, artery clogging, bright yellow brick
we nibbled with crackers. Maybe ironically,
but we ate it.

ELEANOR LERMAN

Beloved

On a steel morning, when the sky is full of wreckage
When it offers a wrecked moon, light seeping from
      the void like gas
you are thrown from your bed again
      by one of those dreams
Arms as thin as paper, shoes a poor excuse,
you shuffle down the boulevards, the ruined lanes
where what is left was finally scattered:
      roses, opals, broken stars
But remember that you have been warned:
keep your head low, your mouth shut
No one has to know that you are as ready
      as you will ever be
Perhaps the city will not forgive you but
      we will, we will

Beloved, yes, it is more than mysterious
Yes, how long we have been waiting
for someone to remember who we are

For the Stay-At-Home Wife

While I am dressing, dream. While I collect my papers
and my courage, stay behind the bright tide of the dawn
and watch the stars wash up like shells upon the shore
Be safe. Be fearless in the silence. Protect the space
        where I should be

And then in green fields, golden fields ribboned with
flowers, go through the open gate. There will be no
wind; the warmth alone will heal you. Ribbons of
light, ribbons of clouds: all this is for you. Stay close
to home. Stay within the loving circle. Far away,
I will write your name between the sun and shadow
        on each page I sign

And when the twilight creeps into the house
with its sad eyes, turn on the lamp. Sit in the chair.
The key is in my pocket and I am coming home
with the news that everything you've lost
remembers you. In time, messages will turn up
in literature and science; in the way the moon
thinks of you when it lingers in the morning, wanting
to wait just one more hour before it is compelled
        to climb back into the dark

FLOWER CONROY

Granting Passage

Leather dark polished
nails behold: me. To your blessing
bestowing mouth.

Therefore I am: crucified-
open, starfish-splayed.
Begging for drink. Begging

for fountain.
Will I or won't I come;
your patient blind-

worming. Can I harness
the redblack sky
of my mind, the red-

black birds
of thought, redblack clouds building
behind my eyelids, the

redblack trees' redblack branches
into my teeth's nerves,
my tongue's dirt road

of taste buds, can I amass
the redblack red, concentrate it
into one flame, one focal point

& hold it
there long enough for
you to cross & cross

the bridge,
that like night, is
this body?

HANNAH BAKER-SIROTY

That One Dream—the Quick of Me.

She approaches me hurried, knows I need
skin. In this instant she must feel the pulse
of my flesh—breasts like clocks, only just
fully wound. The whole of me ticks,
says, *not talk, not talk,* dear god, just take.

Up Here Where the Heat Rises

I dance and my sweat clings—
stays between my breasts and under
wires. Up here, where the heat rises,

it also sticks: holds. So that
the memory of the sweat
and the sweat
are still the same thing
but cooling. Even in winter

this attic will be the hottest place.
It is only
if we make it so. Shake it so. Sway each hip—
and bend at the knee to it. I am only
a dancer and what happens
up here is only music.

HOLLY MITCHELL

We Need the Boat of Love, Not the Boat of Tolerance

We meet our galleries
        between barrels of oil, the photographs

survivors alone in the dark.
        We hear the mermaids

drumming on the bridge, the steel water
        from my childhood sink. We remember quilt

squares sewn unfinished, magic carpets
        sailing on the East River strait. We flow

blood to our Moby Dick of hearts,
        a four-chambered family

of questions in brine. We don't need
        THE BOAT OF TOLERANCE

anchored not far from shore. We won't die
        if this kiss remembers us

from a gutted past. The risk is
        if it forgets our blood, our love

subsumed in the shallow
        alter-world depths, art.

J.K. DANIELS

Genealogy

Under this sun, hung this day so low and close,
you raise your hand to shade your eyes,
which are not suns or jewels but what they are:
brown-gold irises, pupils contracting:
the sun? or are you underwhelmed or angered
by what I've said or done? Might it be my
leg jiggling under this picnic bench or the angle
at which I look like your mother or that phrase
I used that reminds you of my ex, plucking
the fruit from the low-hanging branch? I raise
my hand to better see. In your own created shade,
you say, again, *it's nothing, it's not you; it's me*—and turn
away, lifting your hand from my knee, to give me
your ear, which your genes have carved so delicately.

JANICE GOULD

Waking in the Dark   *For Marta Snow*

Waking in the dark, I lie in bed near the open window
and stare at the sky.

Stars pass by like migrants,
each one bent with a burden of light,
each one murmuring a little song
remembered from childhood.

The road they tread is long, their feet dusty,
hardened by the persistence
and permanence of passage.

Night wind rushes past
cool as velvet, smelling faintly
of lilac and sand.

It nudges the stars along,
and when they begin to wane
whispers encouragement, explaining
the necessity of movement,
proposing a purpose:

that simple relativity sustains us,
that the force of gratitude connects us on our journey,
watchers of skies and stars.

Waking in the dark,
I lie in bed near the open window
and stare at the sky.

Gacela of Bamboo and Plum Blossoms

We were living in a woodcut by Hiroshige
of weathered houses with blue tile roofs, where,
behind a bamboo gate, we found azaleas,
tea roses and jasmine, delicate
and spicy amid stone Buddhas,
placid with their inward gazing.

On the bay a few small boats tilted among whitecaps,
sails open in the fulsome wind.
Across the water the volcano gleamed,
mantled with spruce and incense cedar.
"There is more than one path
to the top of the mountain,"
you remarked, solemn and wistful,
while a flock of blackbirds
alighted in the scraggly pines.

The ocean lapped against the long stretch
of pebbled beaches, mile after mile,
and we knew the piping whales
were rolling, diving on their great migrations,
waving fins at gawking tourists
who huddled on cliffs among parsnips and thistles.
While here, on the steep, winding streets of our city
plum trees blossomed, pink and passionate,
with crooked boughs that smell like imported baskets,
like dyed cloth and paper, like damp gardens.

Far to the west, mist thickened,
clouds churned up, rain came whistling
over the water and poured down upon us—
pushed us into the next panel.

Stumbling, sullen, bent, bedraggled,
I caught at my blowing coat
and looked to find you.
Alas, you had fallen in
with the rabble. Over the arched bridge
you disappeared, jostled but happy
at the foot of the mountain—
dancing in a procession
of drums and gongs.

JOY LADIN

Balance

It's always evening somewhere, and now the evening is mine.
Summer's over, I'm moving on,
the shuddering pans of the scale subside.
I didn't fail, I was right on time,
the perfect balance is undisturbed
by the angst still elbowing on either side.
I'm done with weighing and being weighed. Goodbye!
I soar like a balloon a child let fly.
The little void I held inside
opens into sky.

How Much

I could talk about being sick, but I always talk about being sick,
because I'm always sick, but today I'm sick
and happy, stuffed with fried artichoke, reggiano, gnocchi, and the glow
of knowing my name will be forgotten
when those who knew me are gone,
though of course I'll be remembered by God,
but will God remember the fennel salad and fried rice balls,
the candle on the table reflected in the wine
and the little flame when our fingers brush,
and how much I love the woman who loves me,
how much I love,
how much?

JUDY GRAHN

Magda:

But if you're going to go
dying on your tree
don't forget to come
back to me, give me this

Send me a cloud of birds
messages of mist
and dreams, dreams I can
remember, vivid and real
dreams I can tell

How we used to go strolling
down along the beach
to watch the early morning light
walk upon the water
That's you, I would say, *that's your spell*

As we were talking
you would reach for my hand
you know I can't *stand*
not to see you again
not to feel your body near
not to hear your voice

But I need the choice
not to follow your pain
I want to stay here

for as long as I can
I don't yet want to cross
to wherever you are

Wasn't it bad enough
I had to watch you
meet your nails
wasn't it bitter enough
I had to solace others
over your travails

Wasn't it sad enough
I had to accompany your mother
while we washed you
the prescribed number of times
the prescribed prayers and herbs
I, who never prescribed anything
except you and your words

Don't forget to come back again
don't forget to give me the kiss
to last a lifetime
if you're going to go dying
on your cross
don't forget to come back to me
at least toss me a lifeline
don't just leave me, give me this

LADY MARY WORTLEY MONTAGU

Farewell to Bath

To all you ladies now at Bath,
    And eke, ye beaux, to you,
With aching heart, and wat'ry eyes,
    I bid my last adieu.

Farewell ye nymphs, who waters sip
    Hot reeking from the pumps,
While music lends her friendly aid,
    To cheer you from the dumps.

Farewell ye wits, who prating stand,
    And criticise the fair;
Yourselves the joke of men of sense,
    Who hate a coxcomb's air.

Farewell to Deard's, and all her toys,
    Which glitter in her shop,
Deluding traps to girls and boys,
    The warehouse of the fop.

Lindsay's and Hayes's both farewell,
    Where in the spacious hall,
With bounding steps, and sprightly air,
    I've led up many a ball.

Where Somerville of courteous mien,
    Was partner in the dance,
With swimming Haws, and Brownlow blithe,
    And Britton pink of France.

Poor Nash, farewell! may fortune smile,
    Thy drooping soul revive,
My heart is full I can no more—
    John, bid the coachman drive.

LAURA FOLEY

I Go Down to the River

After making love with a woman

for the first time ever,

I go down to the river where I grew up

and touch it, for the first time ever,

dipping my fingers in the chill East River,

tasting salt from the sea,

as boat-waves flow toward me,

washing over my ankles,

as black-tipped seagulls circle my head.

LESLÉA NEWMAN

I Want to Stay Up Talking But

You kiss me at midnight and tell me to hush
I lie back in bed and do just as you say
Feeling my cheeks and my chest start to blush
You kiss me at midnight and tell me to hush
Then make it quite clear that you're not in a rush
The new year is here and we're happy and gay
You kiss me at midnight and tell me to hush
I lie back in bed and do just as you say

Paradise Found
(for Mary)

Each night at six the hummingbird
drops by our yard, without a word
you stop with hose in hand and freeze
beneath our acorn-laden trees.
The toy bird takes a dainty drink
(you dare not make a sound or blink)
She flits, she flutters—zip!—she's gone
and you come to and carry on.
You snip, you clip, you tend, you hose
each daisy, lily, heather, rose,
then with your strong and gentle hand
you pluck the fairest of the land.
An ordinary eve as this
could bear not one more drop of bliss.

MARINA TSVETAEVA

from Podruga (Friend)

What did you think—in your gray fox, and me
in sable, snowflakes sticking like little lights—
as we searched the Christmas bazaar for bright
ribbons? I stuffed myself on three,

no six, of those pink unsweetened waffles,
and got all mawkish and sentimental
when you pretended to catch the tail
of a passing chestnut horse—be careful!

And then that old biddy, cawing like a crow,
who cursed at us for passing up her rags—
what do you think she and those other hags
thought—a couple of crazy girls from Moscow?

When everybody left, running for the tram,
we stepped into the church, just to rest,
and you kept staring—you couldn't resist—
that ancient icon of the Virgin,

her drawn face and sullen eyes,
full of emaciation and blessing,
and the frame with Venus caressing
a chubby cupid with its ties

to the times of Empress Elizabeth.
You dropped my hand and blurted,
"I want her!" and then gently inserted
a long yellow candle into the holder—with

that knowing hand and its opal ring.
Oh, what got into me, what could I do?
I swore I'd steal that icon for you,
I swore that very night I'd bring

it. And so, like a band of marauders
or soldiers—in a rumble of bells and darkness—
innocent as girls in first communion dress,
we broke into the convent guest quarters.

I pledged for you, to grow more beautiful—
until old age. And then I spilled
the salt. Three times you yelled
when I drew the king of hearts, but still

you gave my head a squeeze, and the tips
of my curls felt your fingers trace—
the flower of your brooch touched my face,
the chill enamel on my lips.

How I made your slender finger
scribble up and down my drowsy
cheek—you teased, *my little boy,*
and said how pleased by that you were...

Translated from the Russian by Leonard Kress

MARTY MCCONNELL

Object

The girl in the tie is a boy in the bar light
and everyone in a skirt's got eyes

for her buttons, snug in their sockets,
not one of them threatening

to burst. The light in the bar is the boy
in the girl sickened by lipstick. Every tie

is a slipknot, an unraveling skirt waist.
Her buttons say nothing

about regret or blurred mornings
or what's under the lycra compressing

her chest. The bar in the boy is a pageant
of light, an astonishment of offers, skirts

pressed against the night, each other,
the boy, the boy in the girl in the tie

in the bar, the bar, her buttons, her hands
like her father's, in charge, something

about power, something about
hold me down, something

about our fathers, some light
off her shoulders, some weight

the tie tells our skirts she can shoulder
better than our fathers, better her

than the bar, the night, our astonishment
of want. The boy in the light

is a pageant of buttons she knows
how to fasten in the dark. Escape

is key for the boy girl going home
with a skirt, going into the night

with the bar in her, with her lycra
and watch fob and the tie loose

as a slipknot, after all we're all trying to kill
or marry our fathers and who better

than her, marooned at the bar with all
of his charm and none of his weaponry. What

better home for our want than the night,
her chest, our hands flattened against

the bar, each other, the lights overhead coming on
just as the music's starting to get good.

MARVA ZOHAR

Our Winter

That winter, our winter, your breasts hung from your collarbone
like a white mismatched pair of socks left on the wire.

I remember how your shadow climbed all the way up the ceiling
when you made that first entrance into my trailer.

You took off your uniform like a cucumber peeling itself, your skin
so pale it seemed green.

You said *I'm not going back there if they grab me by my balls.*
I never knew a girl who talked like you.
I bathed you outside with the hose under the winter sun,
and I clothed you.
My own private refugee.

It was unthinkable for you to wear any of my dresses.
I gave you pajamas.
You were happy to wear them regardless of the hour.
You were happy, I think, even though you were very sad.

You made it sound magnificent as if you were running from an
entire army, not just that one officer who liked to grab your ass.

You showed me something about touch—
there was no other way I could have learned,
I wasn't ready to know it, and it hurt.

With money I had saved for the summertime, we bought
two goats from a shepherd in the Valley of the Goddess.
We brought them home hitchhiking. I know that sounds
impossible now, but this is the way that it was.

One was wet with milk, and we named her Frida
because of her eyebrows. The other was pregnant,
and we called her Persephone, but I can't remember why,
no matter how hard I think of it.

At night I smelled the fear dripping from your pores
and guessed the things that were done to you
according to the imprints your tossing and struggling
left on the mattress.

In the morning we tried to milk the goats, our hands
learned the gesture of closing on the warm, grainy sack,
one finger at a time, milk squirting on our smiles.

We packed apples and sandwiches and tea and headed,
the four of us, out to the meadow.

Soon Frida would die of a snake bite. We would carry her heavy
body into the trunk of a borrowed car.
I was laughing so hard my stomach was hurting.

Soon Persephone would be attacked by a pack of wild
dogs. She would deliver two dead baby goats.
The army police would come for you soon.

But that winter, our winter, when morning came we went
out, the four of us, after the milking. There were so many flowers,
it was wasteful, painful to watch.

You just wanted to scream at the earth—
save a little for later, save some for the season of decay.

I knew every new flower was marking the coming of summer,
the annual season of death when the earth aches for rain, and the
generals of the Middle East would start growing impatient.

Everything was so flammable.
Sooner or later a fire would start, and village men would run out
to hit the flames with blankets.

Out of the flames the snakes and scorpions, the yellow
and the black, all of them will come running toward us.

In the warmth of winter sun we cooled our feet in the puddles as if
each foot was a bottle of champagne.
Floating leaves snuck up and touched our skin,
our feet jumping up, startled every time.

We stayed out there in the meadow while the kale and chard in
our garden grew bittersweet. When the jackals called out from the
valley and the sky began to turn, we walked home.

Home—where the long goat tongs would sip water
from rusty pots and we would do our best
with the little human tongs we had been given
to sip all that was ours for sipping
for the duration of our winter.

MARY ELIZABETH COLERIDGE

The Witch

I have walked a great while over the snow,
And I am not tall nor strong.
My clothes are wet, and my teeth are set,
And the way was hard and long.
I have wandered over the fruitful earth,
But I never came here before.
Oh, lift me over the threshold, and let me in at the door!

The cutting wind is a cruel foe.
I dare not stand in the blast.
My hands are stone, and my voice a groan,
And the worst of death is past.
I am but a little maiden still,
My little white feet are sore.
Oh, lift me over the threshold, and let me in at the door!

Her voice was the voice that women have,
Who plead for their heart's desire.
She came—she came—and the quivering flame
Sunk and died in the fire.
It never was lit again on my hearth
Since I hurried across the floor,
To lift her over the threshold, and let her in at the door.

MARY KATHRYN ARNOLD

Christine

> *Ps. 69:33 "For the Lord heareth the poor, and despiseth not his prisoners."*

They say they tie the knot differently
when they hang women. Something about
a quicker death. I brought my imprisoned

mistress a scarf of pongee to tie
round her neck, and a saveloy
to eat, her last meal. My calves were

pockmarked from the nettles I walked
through, the bucolic march on the
way to the jail. Half the crowd watched

her drop, but the other half had
bigger fish to fry. That half hissed
and opened their eyes wide as they

considered how a column shatters,
how many fragments can never equal
a life. They watched the pillar split,

a pure experiment, so far
from the danger across the street.

MIA

The Dog Lover

> *When others asked the truth of me, I was convinced it was not the truth they wanted, but an illusion they could bear to live with.*
> —Anaïs Nin

Driving the Desert Highway
the girl with blond hair and blue eyes
started crying, "Why can't I be enough?"

As if she had rehearsed this line
a thousand times, her voice
on the verge of throwing
itself off a bridge but for all its intent
remained steadfast to the wheel

through the slow traffic that afforded her
this blown-up drama while the dog lover
blew smoke rings out the window

resigned to a long trip. She who was lost
in counting the windmills along the highway
each whoosh of the pillarblades turning
and gathering in an outside force

deep into the generator, into the cathexis
of its electric center, live sparks crackling.

"I just can't love you that way," she said quietly.
So quietly she could have been speaking
to the dust settling in the radiator, or to the
saguaros standing like sentinels, when

what she really meant to say, "I made a mistake,"
recalling the speaker at the seminar with whom
there'd been a few looks and fewer words, but whose lips
had left her unsettled. She couldn't help but stare.

"I wanted to be you," the girlfriend confided at last. Echoing on the
word, *want,* maybe she left out, "with you," but suddenly
it occurred to the dog lover what was whorishly wrong—

The anatomy of *her* mouth   Where words
kept pushing and pushing and falling out.

MINNIE BRUCE PRATT

The Moon, Reading

The moon looks in our bedroom window at us
sometimes. As I lie down beside you she pulls
a silvery sheet over us, and then retreats
to her night-time reading, east to west.
Night after night that bright gaze moves over
us lying under the comfort of being watched over.

The round illuminated magnifying glass
in Mama's hand as she passed into dementia
and understood less and less, her anxious eyes
reading the same line over and over. The moon
that shone in my window when I was little and
supposed to have religion, so I knelt and prayed
to that light, because she looked back at me.

Everything earthly and imperfect changes
under the moon. In this moment beside you
I am perfectly happy, lying in the moon light,
drifting slowly with you into illegible sleep.

The Wood Thrush Sings

A poem for those burdened, and wakeful at night—

At the end of day, at the beginning of night
you lift the bed covers so I can climb in by.
The bed is a cave, the sheets cool as limestone
except where you've warmed the warp and weft.
The bed is a nest we fold ourselves into, belly
to back, knee to kneefold, wristbone to bone.
Our ribs make a boat of the bed to carry us
to a land of dreams, to what will happen next.

At 3 am I wake up, maybe the IRS, the taxes,
or room after room unpacking hundreds of boxes.
If I put each thing in its place, there will be
a place for the boat to land where the clock
doesn't tick, where the body is unlocked
from pain, where the wood thrush sings after rain.

NAOMI REPLANSKY

The Oasis

I thought I held a fruit cupped in my hand.
Its sweetness burst
And loosed its juice. After long traveling,
After so long a thirst,
    I asked myself: Is this a drought-born dream?
    It was no dream.

I thought I slipped into a hidden room
Out of harsh light.
In cushioned dark, among rich furnishings,
There I restored my sight.
    Such luxury could never be for me!
    It was for me.

I thought I touched a mind that fitted mine
As bodies fit,
Angle to curve; and my mind throbbed to feel
The pulsing of that wit.
    This comes too late, I said. It can't be true!
    But it was true.

I thought the desert ended, and I felt
The fountains leap.
Then gratitude could answer gratitude
Till sleep entwined with sleep.
    Despair once cried: No passion's left inside!
    It lied. It lied.

1987

NICOLE BROSSARD

[brushing the song in you]

brushing the song in you
till smooth lively semaphore sounds
signals love or skin of certitude
till dawn till you
feel that blue surfing horizon
retina enlighten

and again
brushing the real in you
so it could if it could

dissolve time
into spacious mysterious sounds
of throat

let me see that translation again
from the angle of ardor

O. AYES

called rush

this was no purple blossom romance, love. it was me, sucking your lips at the bar, on the dance floor. it was you, pinning me against the wall, clasping my hand on the drive home. it was me, asking questions, you, straddling my hips while we lie on the wet grass as the cops drove by and shone a light. it was our laughs that followed, you placing my finger in your mouth, and i noting the deep blue of the moon, the brown gold of your hair in my hands, and again, your voice soothing even the stars.

R. NEMO HILL

The Girls Are In The Trees

Up from a crown of green break free these three
bright blossom-crusted branches, and from these
ascends a music pitched past anarchy:
near dusk, the girls are once more in the trees.
But what apocalypse has moved them so,
what orgy in high heaven, or what riot
they bear impassioned witness to below—
their frenzied warnings can but amplify it.

Mad bird song yields a carnage all its own,
a crop of bruised pink petals, shaken free
from all but color caught by dying sun.
They're falling all around me, voicelessly.
They're floating down. They stain my arms and hands
with drops of angels' blood, paler than man's.

(Petulu, Bali—2000)

From A Man To The Youth He Loves

You say my eyes, receiving winter roses,
tried both to hide *and* tell you what they knew.
This bright banked fire, which flares out and then closes,
this spark my lowered gaze cannot subdue—
recall the course of blossoms brought indoors,
this pale bouquet of orange meteors.

Late in a season whose sole warmth is you
I watch them flame and fade, without regret.
My gaze is level now. I know it's true
that this one bud which wilts, unopened yet,
may prove to be the promise of all pleasure—
of our two hearts, a constant common measure.

You say my eyes, receiving winter roses,
tried both to hide *and* tell you what we knew
already—that a fire there reposes,
late in a season whose bright spark is you.
Like the embers of those orange winter roses,
my gaze is level now. I know what's true.

(for Julian—2007)

RACHEL ROSE

A Wedding Ghazal

A man loves a man in a silent room.
A man holds a man in a breathless room.

What is the price of an afternoon?
A man holds a man in a breathless room.

The light is gone, but a slender moon
sheds its silver in a breathless room.

The day of blessings is coming soon
when boyfriends become husbands in a sanctified room.

What family blessings can shift to make room
for two men vowing true love in a sacred room?

In spirit I walk with you through roses' perfume
as a small girl throws petals in a joyful room.

Take up your pride. Let freedom bloom
as two men become married before a witnessing room.

Let them dance! Let us dance! Let the groom and the groom
love and be cherished in a radiant room.

RENÉE VIVIEN

Sappho's Disdain

You who judge me, for me you are nothing.
I have contemplated the infinite shadows.
I have neither the vanity of your flowers, nor
Fear of your slander.

You can hardly tarnish the piety
Of my passion for the beauty of women,
Changeable as the sunsets of summer,
Rivers, or fires.

Nothing can sully the stunning faces
Brushed by my breath & my broken singing,
Like a statue standing amid the passing,
Soul all serenity.

Translated from the French by Mike Alexander

RICK MULLIN

Recital

One cloud like an adamant balloon ship
came in over Branchport, scudding toward
the bluff, a spacious blue-gray change of weather.

It sprinkled on the Esperanza Mansion,
challenging the map of lily fronds
that mirrored in the lake all afternoon
like Queen Anne's lace. A scow that rolled to cover
half the sky with something like a welcome
dread advanced as I stood in recital
underneath a silver maple on the lawn.

"Three perfect days" she'd sighed and sipped her wine
before abandoning her wicker throne
dead-center on the lofting grass to take a nap
above the tree where I had come to read aloud.

Keuka Lake, August 8, 2012

RISA DENENBERG

Yellow Star

In my case, the yellow star
will be made of two perfect pink triangles,
cut from cheap dry goods at the Triangle Shirtwaist Factory
where the women
sew stars on at the ready
hunched over their Singers
and, not wasting time on stairs,
work right up until closing time, then jump.

They didn't want to die so young
and neither did the gay boys who died in droves
at the close of last century. I would be one
who would beg you to shoot me,
who would know that borders lie,
that I could not endure the march through the woods
in the snow to the trains at the end.

We who say never forget
also know that it could happen again
to us
and we do not know more now
about how to make it stop.

The stitching never ends. For practice,
I have sutured my arm to my sleeve
with triangles made from pages torn
from the Book of Job.

Before world

Birds don't sing. Jazz doesn't sing. And then
birds teach hominids to jazz.

Before trees, goats don't climb trees and trees don't bare
leaves. And then, trees teach birds to nest.

Before seas, men don't build boats. Life swims before
it flies. And then, birds teach frogs to hop.

Before fences, coyotes don't kill chickens. And then
earth is partitioned and frogs teach girls to skip rope.

And when I unearth your face like sun-scorched earth,
the sun hides her face. And then faith restores the sun.

Before faith of words is faith of trees. And songs sing
before sin. And then songs teach us to pray.

Before prayer Negroes don't swing from trees. Landmines
don't amputate boys. And then prayers teach hate.

When women sing, the wind sails free
through trees and makes love to the sea.

RITA MAE REESE

At 36, Hulga Speaks of Love

In wine is truth and in rum freedom,
      the freedom to get up from the porch
  with her mother still talking.
In rum is the Judge in her room,
      sitting beside the books behind glass.
  Love should be full of anger, he intones,
      and she nods, sits on the bed, takes off her shoes.
Judge weighs evidence against Hulga day and night,
      mostly night.

Love, she repeats, but behind her absent gaze
      at the saint in the corner
  she is *parting a pink gold shower of hair,*
      dividing it upon a back bare its length.
  She had thought she was all done with asking
but in rum is (God help her) the consent to love.

In rum is a radio playing
      so far away she can't make out the tune,
  a shadow of sound slipping toward Hulga
      through years and hundreds of miles
  from the girl in the apartment downstairs.
This the only music she listens to.

She is *bending to kiss exactly the hollow of her back,*
exactly the spot
best suited to receive first [her] lips
and then [her] cheek.
Love, and *do* what you like, he mutters. Hulga is
multiplied by the dozens of women
she has never seduced. She is cast into a legion of swine
sailing over a cliff.   And she is flying.

ROBIN BECKER

The Black Bear Inside Me

All summer I elude them—
who think they want to see my

three cubs someone
said she spotted

on the gravel road that severs
thick woods

near a row of mailboxes,
by the stream;

who take the path down
and up the mowing

with baskets on their arms,
fearful

when they hear me
huff or blow.

They know
I will outrun, outswim,

outclimb, bluff-charge,
and in winter

drop my heart rate
from 40 to 8 beats a minute

in my den of
wind-thrown trees.

They know they will take
me in the September

kill, harvesting
my kind with dogs

and guns, and they know
we haven't taken one of them

since 1784 in this state
where 5,000 black bear

clear carcasses
of deer and moose

and sow
fruit trees and shrubs.

They know they need us
who are so like them

our numbers tell
the story, yes, the land

that supports us
supports them; without us,

adapted to scarcity and woodland
loss, they're going down.

ROSE KELLEHER

Compensation

The blind can hear things other people can't,
one sense allowed to cover for the other
as if some slipshod god were keeping count,
half-trying to be fair. I know I'd rather
have seeing eyes than echometric ears,

but then, I know the awkward and unlovely
acquire fantastic powers after years
of practice in the art of being lonely;
conjuring wine from water, bread from stone,
wringing pleasures from the empty air
you with your luck in love could not imagine;

blessed—like saints in furnaces, withstanding
heat that would burn beauty to the bone—
with gifts they didn't ask for, and can't share.

SARA TEASDALE

Since There Is No Escape

Since there is no escape, since at the end
    My body will be utterly destroyed,
This hand I love as I have loved a friend,
    This body I tended, wept with and enjoyed;
Since there is no escape even for me
    Who love life with a love too sharp to bear:
The scent of orchards in the rain, the sea
    And hours alone too still and sure for prayer—
Since darkness waits for me, then all the more
Let me go down as waves sweep to the shore
    In pride, and let me sing with my last breath;
In these few hours of light I lift my head;
Life is my lover—I shall leave the dead
    If there is any way to baffle death.

September Midnight

Lyric night of the lingering Indian Summer,
Shadowy fields that are scentless but full of singing,
Never a bird, but the passionless chant of insects,
    Ceaseless, insistent.

The grasshopper's horn, and far-off, high in the maples,
The wheel of a locust leisurely grinding the silence
Under a moon waning and worn, broken,
    Tired with summer.

Let me remember you, voices of little insects,
Weeds in the moonlight, fields that are tangled with asters,
Let me remember, soon will the winter be on us,
    Snow-hushed and heavy.

Over my soul murmur your mute benediction,
While I gaze, O fields that rest after harvest,
As those who part look long in the eyes they lean to,
    Lest they forget them.

SARAH SARAI

Longing for a Blue Sky

I am goal-oriented like an orgasm,
exhausted already by details of your ego.
My details are colored "hesitation" and "confidence?"
though age, she educates.

My mood is London longing for a blue sky.
I take the Hudson River as my lover
the Southwest as my comforter
Mount Shasta as my tomb.
Who wouldn't want to spend millennia
in a fine female breast?

In my pain—everything I need to be pleased.
I am pleased already, could you shut up!
See me, in a woman's burial mound?
About your ego:
It destroys nothing, not even itself.

This Way and That

It was a fairy funeral. [William Blake]

On the garden bed of
Blake's fairy procession
roll this and that, these ways
of midnight pleasure

in enchantment and
commonplace wisdom
like don't touch the fairies,
they're sensitive.

Act within a soul
populated by
sightings and wistful affection,

see the filmstrip is at
high-enough speed
life's fluidity's felt,
as at the funeral Blake saw,

a bodylet laid out on a leaf.
Authentication enough for me
[that fairies exist] I e-mailed you
who reminded me
Blake saw God when he was

four. God got down on Her
omniaching knees
now and then to spy on
William Blake
and could hardly contain Her

infinite self, waiting for
the artist to become Heaven and
those paintings to be flashed to
the good and bad alike as proof of

the great mystery of vision
even She can't figure out.

SHAWNDRA MILLER

Freeze Warning, April 10

All day I have hunkered indoors, moving words about on a screen,
twiddling through papers—while outside Life
springs forth in its calamitous way, shedding pollen, fur, seeds,
feathers, petals, petiole and leaf:
making way for more Life and more.
As evening sinks into blue splendor I walk the neighborhood,
my dog springing just shy of the end of the leash.
The wind has February teeth, but everywhere is soft Ireland green.
I pass the boy playing a solitary game of hoops.
His bare limbs are an elbow jabbed straight into the throat
of Freeze Warning. He angles under the basket, lets one fly,
showboating for the trees or, perhaps, for an unseen father's appraisal.
His mother's newly planted beds are shrouded for the night,
buds veiled under frayed sheets dotted with counterfeit blossoms.
I turn toward home, tugging my wool cap
lower over my ears. On the corner
Roseanne is tending to her cottage garden. (Inside I quail;
I have been afraid of her eyes
ever since my crime of indifference 13 years ago—police cars
at her house, back door kicked in, me on my porch pretending
not to notice—now I expect her gaze to cut me.) So here
she is on the sidewalk, shears drooping to the earth,
holding an armful of burgundy blooms,
and I say, "Are those peonies? This early! They're gorgeous,"
meeting their velvet faces more easily than hers, and she tells me
about her adored tree peony, which flowers early every year.
"And they smell so good." She holds

the bouquet out, inviting my lean and whiff. (Like cardamom, citrus,
soil, a bite to my nostrils.) We talk about Freeze Warning, about nature
running ahead of the season, about the coming night, a threat
to the tenderest plants, but on our faces are smiles, and we shrug:
What can you do? Walking home with feet stirring pale dogwood petals,
maple samaras, strings of yellow oak pollen, I leave
a carapace of my own in pieces on the street: pieces weightless enough
to be scoured away by the cold wind of Freeze Warning.

Blackbird

In the blue ocean-sky above the Great Basin
swim birds who own immensity,
their hollow bones and feathers made to rise,
to know the far horizon.

Still some are otherwise inclined.

A blackbird lights on the rent screen of my door, his daily visit.
He's torn the mesh to make a parted curtain, a raveled lectern—
this hole the work of weeks or more.
He all but clears his throat, then:
His first note fogs the glass with hot beak breath.
His shoulder blazes quiver at the trill.

He taps his bill on the glass.

I think he means to strike an enemy only he can see.
Will he work the glass till it too cracks under his beak?
Each day he turns his back to the blue,
chooses to pick at his own image
while just behind him breathes infinitude.

What say you, Blackbird? Your song's in my ears from dawn to dusk.

Do you call me to hammer an opening
of my own making? Or do you mirror my foolish face,
reflecting made-up threats I cannot quash
while ocean-sky—my birthright too—invites me, laden as I am,
to swim for that horizon?

SOPHIE JEWETT

Defeated

When the last fight is lost, the last sword broken;
The last call sounded, the last order spoken;
When from the field where braver hearts lie sleeping,
Faint, and athirst, and blinded, I come creeping,
With not one waving shred of palm to bring you,
With not one splendid battle-song to sing you,
O Love, in my dishonor and defeat,
Your measureless compassion will be sweet.

SUZANNE J. DOYLE

Some Sleep Deeper

Lean as the whippets you would keep and strung
Taut as some ancient huntress' bow,
You move to stretch your long, tormented bones
And dream the barren country we both know.

The altars there receive the very young
Who lust after the purity of stone:
The dry creek bed of seasons passed alone,
Atoning for a crime that's not your own.
But something lies in wait and lures you on,
Along the subtle path that keeps you narrow,
And there, before your own lithe arm is drawn,
Swift beauty rifts you cleaner than an arrow:
The small song of a thrush dies in the brake,
The snake recoils its colors in the cave,
The saffron light a bend of willows shake
Abandon you to all the life you crave.

Beside me now you burn, white as the moon,
Prepared for some sleep deeper than I dare,
While I insist you'll grow to love me soon,
Forgetting all I know of being there.

SUZANNE GARDINIER

89

The vase of tower fragments and his mother's
last dress made ashes the wind blows loose

How the rain reaches into the winter ground
and warms and turns the grasses loose

Walk on your knees says the guard to his father
Give me a name and I'll turn you loose

The harbormaster's hands in the morning
on the knots the night tides tried to pull loose

The peony petals pressed in round bud
then unfolding Your shirt's pink Then falling loose

How the years found what she held so tightly
and took it Prying her fingers loose

Left in the tree he passed every day
A man The tatters of his clothes flapping loose

The smallness of the barbarians' airplanes
after the emperor's airplanes let loose

How he sat coughing shards of his nation's hatred
How she wanted to keep him and he said Turn me loose

The meadow paddock by the intransigent
sea broken open and the horses run loose

She's remembering your way with her bindings
Yrs bridled How you tighten How you cut them loose

TIMOTHY MURPHY

An Old Man Speaks

You haven't found me frothing on the floor
and bleeding from the tongue for a long time.
You are my weekly visitor. The door
creaks open, and a corpse dusted with lime
revives to smile. Danny, had I been straight,
I might be you, smothered in happiness,
children swarming my knees. But I've a fate,
Dom in the Anglo Saxon, and I'd guess
the All Father has placed me on this path
diverging in a leafless wood, to find
some way to charity, away from wrath.
My eyes are bandaged, so I'm choosing blind
between two destinations: Heaven, Hell.
Visit me here, and try to love me well.

ABOUT THE POETS

Mary Kathryn Arnold writes in Halifax, Nova Scotia, where she lives with her wife. Her work has appeared in Canada and the United States in journals such as *Arc Poetry Magazine, The Fiddlehead, Mezzo Cammin,* and *The Antigonish Review.*

O. Ayes is a queer writer who has taught at universities in St. Louis and New York City, as well as international schools in Tanzania and Indonesia. Her writing appears on *The Manhattanville Review, LEVELER, T/OUR, Sukoon, The Nervous Breakdown, Matador, Five Quarterly, Blackbird,* and elsewhere.

Hannah Baker-Siroty is an Assistant Professor of Writing at Pine Manor College. She has degrees from the University of Wisconsin-Madison and Sarah Lawrence College. Some of her work can be found in *Best New Poets 2012, Cactus Heart,* and *Lumina.* She is currently writing poems about the Vice Presidents of the United States. Learn more at www.poetrying.com.

Robin Becker, Liberal Arts Research Professor of English and Women's Studies at Penn State, has published seven collections of poems, five in the University of Pittsburgh Press Poetry series. Her most recent, *Tiger Heron,* appeared in 2014. Becker serves as Contributing and Poetry Editor for *The Women's Review of Books* for which she writes a column on contemporary poetry called "Field Notes."

Nicole Brossard, born in Montréal, has published more than thirty books and received many awards, including the Governor General, twice, for her poetry. She codirected the film *Some American Feminists* and coedited *Anthologie de la poésie des femmes au Québec.* Her work has been widely translated. Her most recent book of poems translated into English is *White Piano.*

Mary Elizabeth Coleridge (1861-1907) was a precocious and prolific writer of poems, essays, and novels. She never married and taught grammar and literature to young women.

Flower Conroy is the author of three chapbooks, *Escape to Nowhere* (Rain Mountain Press), *The Awful Suicidal Swans* (Headmistress Press), and *Facts About Snakes & Hearts*, which won Heavy Feather Review's chapbook contest. She is the winner of Radar Poetry's first annual Coniston Prize, selected by Mary Biddinger. Her poetry is forthcoming/has appeared in *American Literary Review*, *Jai Alia*, and other journals.

J.K. Daniels's poems have appeared in *Queer South; Calyx; Best New Poets, 2011; Beltway Poetry Quarterly;* and others. She has an M.F.A. from George Mason University and teaches creative writing and literature at Northern Virginia Community College.

Catherine Breese Davis (1924-2002), against terrible odds, studied with the best-known poets of her time, held a Stegner fellowship, and self-published four books. A collection of her poems, *Catherine B. Davis: On the Life and Work of an American Master*, edited by Martha Collins, Kevin Prufer, and Martin Rock, is forthcoming from the Pleiades Unsung Masters Series in 2015.

Risa Denenberg is a cofounder of Headmistress Press and earns her keep as a nurse practitioner in Sequim, Washington. She has published three chapbooks, *what we owe each other* & *In My Exam Room* (The Lives You Touch Publications) and *blinded by clouds* (Hyacinth Girls Press); and a full-length collection, *Mean Distance from the Sun* (Aldrich Press).

Suzanne J. Doyle has published the following slim volumes of verse: *Sweeter for the Dark* (1982), *Domestic Passions* (1984), *Dangerous Beauties* (1990), and *Calypso* (2003). For more than 25 years she has made her living writing and editing for high-tech clients in Silicon Valley, California.

Andrea Dulanto is a Latina lesbian writer. Degrees include an M.F.A. in Creative Writing from Florida International University, and a B.A. in Literature and Women's Studies from Antioch College in Ohio. Publications include *Berkeley Poetry Review*, *Court Green*, and *Sinister Wisdom*. andreadulanto.wordpress.com

LAURA FOLEY is the author of four poetry collections, including *Joy Street* and *The Glass Tree*. She lives with her partner Clara Gimenez and their three dogs on a woody hill in Vermont. For book information or more poems, please visit laurafoley.net

SUZANNE GARDINIER is the author of four books of poetry, most recently *Iridium & Selected Poems 1986-2009*, & a book of essays on poetry & politics called *A World That Will Hold All the People*. She's received awards from the New York Foundation for the Arts & the Lannan Foundation. She teaches writing at Sarah Lawrence College & lives in Manhattan & Havana.

JANICE GOULD is Koyoonk'auwi (Concow). She is the Pike's Peak Poet Laureate for 2014-2016 and has earned NEA and Astraea Foundation awards. Her most recent book, *Doubters and Dreamers,* was a Colorado Book Award Finalist and a Milt Kessler Book Award Finalist. She is an Associate Professor in Women's and Ethnic Studies at the University of Colorado.

JUDY GRAHN is a poet, writer, and philosopher (of Metaformia). She has published 13 woman-centered books, marched for Gay Rights in 1965, and holds many literary awards. Publisher's Triangle established a Judy Grahn Nonfiction Award. She was Lifetime Achievement Grand Marshall of the San Francisco Gay Pride Parade in 2014; is currently an independent Professor-at-Large.

ALIX GREENWOOD is a Lesbian living in Oakland, California ("Night" was written before the Great California Drought!). Her poems have appeared in *Sinister Wisdom, Rain and Thunder,* and *Three Line Poetry.*

R. NEMO HILL is the author of a novel, *Pilgrim's Feather* (Quantuck Lane); a poem based on an H.P Lovecraft story, *The Strange Music of Erich Zann* (Hippocampus Press); a chapbook, *Prolegomena To An Essay On Satire* (Modern Metrics); and a collection of poems, *When Men Bow Down* (Dos Madres Press). He is the editor of EXOT BOOKS (www.exot.typepad.com/exotbooks).

Sophie Jewett (1861-1909) taught English at Wellesley College and wrote poems about intimacy between women.

Rose Kelleher is the author of *Bundle o' Tinder* (Anthony Hecht Prize) and *Native Species*. Her poems and essays have appeared in many online and print journals.

Alyse Knorr is the author of *Copper Mother* (Switchback Books, 2015), *Annotated Glass* (Furniture Press Books, 2013) and the chapbook *Alternates* (Dancing Girl Press, 2014). She received her MFA from George Mason University. She serves as a founding co-editor of Gazing Grain Press and teaches at the University of Alaska Anchorage.

Joy Ladin is the author of six books of poetry; her seventh collection, *Impersonation,* is due out in 2015. Her work has been recognized with a Fulbright Scholarship. She holds the David and Ruth Gottesman Chair in English at Stern College of Yeshiva University.

Eleanor Lerman is the author of six books of poetry, most recently *Strange Life*. She was named a Guggenheim Fellow; was a National Book Award finalist; received grants from The New York Foundation for the Arts, a fellowship from the National Endowment for the Arts and won the Lenore Marshall Prize. Her second novel, *Radiomen,* was published in January 2015.

Amy Levy (1861-1889) was a gifted writer and pioneering feminist. She fell in love with Vernon Lee, and they both wrote works with lesbian themes. When Levy committed suicide, Oscar Wilde wrote her obituary.

Amy Lowell (1874-1925) wrote "some of the most remarkable, barely encoded, lesbian poems since Sappho." (Lillian Faderman) She was wealthy, and lived in a Boston marriage with her muse, Ada Dwyer Russell.

Marty McConnell lives in Chicago and received her MFA from Sarah Lawrence College. Her work has recently appeared in *Best American Poetry 2014, Southern Humanities Review, Gulf Coast,* and *Indiana Review*. Her first full-length collection, "wine for a shotgun," was published in 2012 by EM Press. martyoutloud.com

Colleen McKee is the author of four books and chapbooks. Her most recent book is a collection of poetry, memoir, and fiction called *Nine Kinds of Wrong* (JKP, 2013). She also likes to make miniature abstract artworks; one appeared in *Lavender Review* in 2014. Her work is forthcoming in *Oakland Review*. Ninekindsofwrong.blogspot.com

Charlotte Mew (1869-1928) was publicly mocked for her love for women, but praised by Virginia Woolf, who called her "the greatest living poetess." In 1928, the year of the obscenity trial for *The Well of Loneliness,* Mew burned most of her poems and committed suicide.

Mia was born in Korea and grew up in Ohio and Texas. She moved to California after graduating from the University of Texas at Austin. She now resides in the suburbs of Denver. Mia used to edit the online magazine, *Tryst,* which has been on an extended hiatus. The poetry will always be there.

Shawndra Miller, Mennonite by birth, mystic by nature, is a writer who lives in Indianapolis. Her work has appeared in *Farm Indiana, Acres USA, The Boiler Journal,* and other periodicals. She is currently working on a nonfiction book about community resilience, while blogging about the world's remaking at shawndramiller.com

Holly Mitchell is a poet and writer from Kentucky. Her work can be found in *Lavender Review, Ishaan Review, the Suburban Review* blog, *Split Quarterly,* and *The Bakery,* among other journals. Holly studied at Mount Holyoke College and currently lives in New York City.

Lady Mary Wortley Montagu (1689-1762) was a prolific writer skewered by Pope and Walpole; an aristocrat banished from the royal court for her satirical verse; and a traveler whose detailed descriptions of nude Turkish women inspired a painting by Ingres.

Rick Mullin is a poet, painter, and journalist living in Northern New Jersey. His book, *Sonnets from the Voyage of the Beagle,* was published by Dos Madres Press, Loveland, Ohio, in 2014. Dos Madres also published his collection, *Coelacanth* (2013), and his epic poem *Soutine* (2012). His booklength poem *Huncke* was published by Seven Towers, Dublin, Ireland, in 2010.

Tim Murphy has over 800 poems in print, and he is the author of a dozen books. He hunts in North Dakota.

Lesléa Newman is the author of 65 books for readers of all ages including *October Mourning: A Song for Matthew Shepard.* Her literary awards include poetry fellowships from the NEA and the Massachusetts Artists Foundation. From 2008-2010 she served as the poet laureate of Northampton, MA. Her newest poetry collection, *I Carry My Mother,* was published by Headmistress Press in 2015.

Minnie Bruce Pratt, writer and activist, came out as a lesbian in North Carolina in 1975 and now lives in Syracuse, NY. She received a Lambda Literary Award for *The Dirt She Ate: Selected and New Poems,* and the Audre Lorde Award for Poetry from the Publishing Triangle for *Inside the Money Machine.* Her poems, *Crime Against Nature*, about losing custody of her children as a lesbian mother, were recently re-issued by Sinister Wisdom/Midsummer Night's Press.

Rita Mae Reese is the author of *The Alphabet Conspiracy* (2011) and *The Book of Hulga,* which won the Felix Pollak Prize and will be published by the University of Wisconsin Press in 2016. She has received numerous awards, including a "Discovery"/The Nation award and a Rona Jaffe Foundation Writers' Award.

NAOMI REPLANSKY was born in 1918 and lives in New York. *Ring Song* (Scribner, 1952) was a finalist for the National Book Award in poetry. Her *Collected Poems* (Godine/Black Sparrow, 2012) won the William Carlos Williams award of the Poetry Society of America and was a finalist for Poets' Prize. Her partner is the writer Eva Kollisch.

RACHEL ROSE's most recent book, *Song & Spectacle* (2012) won the Audre Lorde Poetry Award in the U.S. and the Pat Lowther Award in Canada. She is the winner of the Peterson Memorial Prize for poetry and the Bronwen Wallace award for fiction, and the recipient of a 2014 Pushcart Prize. She is the Poet Laureate of Vancouver for 2014-2017.

CHRISTINA ROSSETTI (1830-1894) never married, worked with unwed mothers and fallen women, and wrote technically masterful and musical, sexually charged poems about women.

SAPPHO translator BRIAN CARR currently lives in Jackson, Wyoming with his wife and son. In addition to writing and classical scholarship, Brian is a career firefighter/ paramedic with Jackson Hole Fire/EMS. He also heads a scholarly outreach organization, AOTON (aoton.org).

SARAH SARAI's poems are in *Pool Poetry, Thrush, Yew, Posit, Ascent, Threepenny Review, The Writing Disorder, Fairy Tale Review, Boston Review, Say It Loud: Poems About James Brown* (Whirlwind), *The OR Panthology: Ocellus Reseau* (Other Rooms), and others. Her collection, *The Future Is Happy*, was published by BlazeVOX. She lives in New York.

E.F. SCHRAEDER's creative work has appeared in *Hoax, Voluted Tales, Siren's Call, Mused, Clare Literary Journal,* and other journals and anthologies. A contributor to the nonfiction anthologies *Kicked Out* and the forthcoming *Queering Sexual Violence,* Schraeder is also the author of a poetry chapbook, *The Hunger Tree.*

Sara Teasdale (1884-1933) is a neglected, significant American poet who loved women and committed suicide.

Marina Tsvetaeva (1892-1941) translator Leonard Kress has published poetry and fiction in *Massachusetts Review, Iowa Review, Crab Orchard Review, American Poetry Review, Harvard Review,* etc. His recent collections are *The Orpheus Complex, Living in the Candy Store,* and *Braids & Other Sestinas*. He teaches philosophy, religion, and creative writing at Owens College in Ohio.

Ann Tweedy's first chapbook, *Beleaguered Oases,* was published by tcCreativePress in 2010, and her second chapbook, *White Out,* was published by Green Fuse Press in June 2013. Her poetry has appeared in *Clackamas Literary Review, Rattle, damselfly press, literary mama,* and elsewhere. In addition to writing poetry and essays, she is also a law professor and a practicing attorney.

Renée Vivien (1877-1909) translator Mike Alexander's first full-length collection, RETROgrade was published by P & J Poetics, LLC. His chapbook, *We Internet in Different Voices* (Modern Metrics), is available through EXOT books. His poems have appeared in *River Styx, Borderlands, Bateau, Abridged, Measure, Shit Creek Review, Raintown Review* & other journals.

Marva Zohar has practiced midwifery in the U.S., Uganda, and Israel. She is currently completing her MFA in poetry at Bar-Ilan University with an emphasis in poetry documenting gender-based violence. She is the winner of the 2013 Andrea Moriah Memorial Prize in Poetry and lives in Jaffa, Israel, by the sea.

www.ingramcontent.com/pod-product-compliance
Lightning Source LLC
Chambersburg PA
CBHW071233090426
42736CB00014B/3069